W9-BEW-323

U.S. PRESIDENTIAL ELECTIONS: HOW THEY WORK

VOTING FOR THE PRESIDENT OF THE UNITED STATES

SHANNON H. HARTS

PowerKiDS
press

New York

Published in 2020 by The Rosen Publishing Group, Inc.
29 East 21st Street, New York, NY 10010

Copyright © 2020 by The Rosen Publishing Group, Inc.

All rights reserved. No part of this book may be reproduced in any form without permission in writing from the publisher, except by a reviewer.

First Edition

Editor: Rachel Gintner
Book Design: Tanya Dellaccio

Photo Credits: Cover Hill Street Studios/DigitalVision/Getty Images; p. 5 John Parrot/Stocktrek Images/ Getty Images; p. 6 https://upload.wikimedia.org/wikipedia/commons/9/9d/Scene_at_the_ Signing_of_the_Constitution_of_the_United_States.jpg; p. 7 https://upload.wikimedia.org/wikipedia/ commons/9/90/United_States_House_of_Representatives_chamber.jpg; pp. 9 (top), 14 Universal History Archive/Universal Images Group/Getty Images; p. 9 (bottom) https://upload.wikimedia.org/wikipedia/ commons/c/c7/National_Women%27s_Suffrage_Association.jpg; p. 10 Bettman/Getty Images; p. 11 Robert W. Kelley/The LIFE Picture Collection/Getty Images; p. 13 hermosawave/iStock/Getty Images Plus/Getty Images; p. 15 Chicago History Museum/Archive Photos/Getty Images; p. 17 (top) Joseph Sohm/Shutterstock.com; p. 17 (bottom) Joe Raedle/Getty Images News/Getty Images; p. 19 Joshua Lott/ Getty Images News/Getty Images; p. 21 (top) Geroge Frey/Getty Images News/Getty Images; p. 21 (bottom) Justin Sullivan/Getty Images News/Getty Images; pp. 23, 27 Stephen Maturen/Getty Images News/Getty Images; p. 24 BILL WECHTER/AFP/Getty Images; p. 25 JOSEPH PREZIOSO/AFP/Getty Images; p. 29 Bloomberg/Getty Images.

Cataloging-in-Publication Data

Names: Harts, Shannon H.
Title: Voting for the president of the United States / Shannon H. Harts.
Description: New York : PowerKids Press, 2020. | Series: U.S. presidential elections: how they work | Includes glossary and index.
Identifiers: ISBN 9781725311022 (pbk.) | ISBN 9781725311046 (library bound) | ISBN 9781725311039 (6 pack)
Subjects: LCSH: Voting–United States–Juvenile literature. | Elections–United States–Juvenile literature.
Classification: LCC JK1978.H36 2020 | DDC 324.6'50973–dc23

Manufactured in the United States of America

CPSIA Compliance Information: Batch # CWPK20. For Further Information contact Rosen Publishing, New York, New York at 1-800-237-9932.

CONTENTS

POWER TO THE PEOPLE

Let's journey back in time to the end of the American Revolution in 1783, when the British colonies beat immense odds to win freedom from Great Britain. Although it was a time of celebration, many believed there was a much tougher battle ahead: governing without a king. Fast-forward over 230 years without a king, and the United States is considered one of the world's most powerful nations.

Voting is an important part of keeping this nation and its **democracy** strong. It allows you to pick a leader that you believe will make the best choices for the country's future. Thomas Jefferson, one of the nation's Founding Fathers and the third president, once said: "We do not have government by the majority. We have government by the majority who participate."

PATH TO THE PRESIDENCY

TO BE PRESIDENT, YOU MUST BE AT LEAST 35 YEARS OLD, HAVE LIVED IN THE UNITED STATES FOR AT LEAST 14 YEARS, AND BE A NATURAL BORN CITIZEN OR BORN IN THE UNITED STATES.

WHAT POWERS DO PRESIDENTS HAVE?

GEORGE WASHINGTON'S EXAMPLE LED TO THE 22ND **AMENDMENT**, PREVENTING PRESIDENTS FROM SERVING MORE THAN TWO TERMS. DURING THIS TIME THEY:

- ACT AS COMMANDER IN CHIEF OF THE ARMED FORCES
- NOMINATE THE HEADS OF GOVERNMENT DEPARTMENTS, FEDERAL JUDGES, AND SUPREME COURT JUSTICES
- CAN GRANT PARDONS FOR FEDERAL OFFENSES
- CAN ASSEMBLE CONGRESS IN SPECIAL SESSIONS, OR MEETINGS
- RECEIVE AMBASSADORS
- CAN ISSUE EXECUTIVE ORDERS
- CAN MAKE TREATIES WITH SENATE APPROVAL
- CAN VETO, OR REJECT, LAWS APPROVED BY CONGRESS

This painting shows New York City crowds in 1783 cheering for George Washington—who later became the first U.S. president—and his men, after they won the American Revolution.

THE WINNING PROPOSAL

Even after defeating Great Britain, the nation's founders had a major job ahead of them in deciding how the new country would be run. When the delegates met in Philadelphia for the **Constitutional Convention** in 1787, one of the first popular ideas was that Congress would elect the nation's president. But it was feared this would offset the balance of power between the three governmental branches.

The Founding Fathers, shown below at the Constitutional Convention, created the Electoral College as the body that officially elects the president and vice president of the United States.

THERE ARE 538 ELECTORS IN THE ELECTORAL COLLEGE. A MAJORITY, OR 270 ELECTORAL VOTES, IS NEEDED TO WIN THE PRESIDENTIAL ELECTION. A STATE'S ELECTORS ARE THE SAME AS THE NUMBER OF MEMBERS IN ITS CONGRESSIONAL DELEGATION. THERE'S ONE ELECTOR FOR EACH MEMBER IN THE HOUSE OF REPRESENTATIVES AND TWO FOR THE SENATORS.

PATH TO THE PRESIDENCY

IN 1789, ONLY ABOUT 6 PERCENT OF THE POPULATION OF THE U.S. COULD VOTE—ONLY WHITE MEN OVER THE AGE OF 21 WHO OWNED LAND.

While it was also suggested the nation's people select the president directly via a popular vote, others worried citizens might not know enough about politics to make such an important decision, and they could be too focused on matters close to their homes. Much debate continued until a proposal for the Electoral College received the most support.

LIBERTY FOR ALL— MAKING IT REAL

In 1776, John Adams—who'd one day be president—was heading to the Continental Congress where the Declaration of Independence would be signed when he received a letter from his wife, Abigail. She asked him to "remember the ladies" while creating the new nation's framework. Women's voices were almost entirely left out of most of the nation's political decision-making. Still, women such as Abigail Adams wanted more equality for women in government. Eventually, in July 1848, the women's suffrage movement was born at a convention in Seneca Falls, New York.

The movement saw the creation of many groups aimed at securing women's suffrage, or the right to vote. After years of protests, finally, in 1920, the state of Tennessee—by one vote—was the 36th state to approve the 19th Amendment, which gave all women the right to vote.

Susan B. Anthony and Elizabeth Cady Stanton formed the National Woman Suffrage Association in 1869. ▶

SUSAN B. ANTHONY

ELIZABETH CADY STANTON

VOTES FOR WOMEN

NATIONAL WOMAN SUFFRAGE ASSOCIATION

MARSHAL

The 15th Amendment gave African American men the right to vote in 1870 after the bloody U.S. Civil War. But their true battle for equality was far from over. **Discriminatory** practices prevented many African American men from voting. These included poll taxes, literacy tests, **fraud**, and **intimidation**.

STILL WORK TO DO: *SHELBY COUNTY V. HOLDER*

THE 2013 U.S. SUPREME COURT CASE *SHELBY COUNTY V. HOLDER* SAW THE COURT **INVALIDATE** THE WAY STATES' POLICIES, UNDER SECTION 5 OF THE VOTING RIGHTS ACT, ARE DETERMINED. SECTION 5 REQUIRED CERTAIN AREAS WITH A HISTORY OF LIMITING VOTING TO BRING ANY PROPOSED CHANGE IN THEIR VOTING PRACTICES TO A FEDERAL COURT OR THE U.S. DEPARTMENT OF JUSTICE. THIS HAD EFFECTIVELY BLOCKED LAWS THAT MADE IT HARDER TO VOTE. NOW, MANY STATES ARE PRESSING CONGRESS TO IMPROVE THIS PROTECTION TO STRENGTHEN THE VOTING RIGHTS ACT.

VOTERS OFTEN FIND MORE THAN JUST CANDIDATES ON THEIR BALLOTS. THEY ALSO FIND POLICY PROPOSALS AROUND IMPORTANT ISSUES.

Martin Luther King Jr. led a massive march on Washington, D.C., in 1963 to achieve civil rights, including equal voting rights.

Many courageous people marched, protested, and were even arrested to put an end to the unfair treatment. In 1963 and 1964, Dr. Martin Luther King Jr. brought hundreds to courthouses in Selma, Alabama, to register to vote. The Voting Rights Act of 1965 aimed to prevent voting obstacles by banning literacy tests and the use of poll taxes, among other policies. However, following a 2013 Supreme Court decision, parts of this act are not in use today.

WHO CAN VOTE TODAY

Thanks to numerous amendments, laws, and battles, voting is open to many more people than when the United States was born. Two of the most important qualifications for voting are that you must be a U.S. citizen and at least 18 years of age before Election Day. Article I, Section 4 of the Constitution states, "Congress may at any time by law make or alter such regulations" governing elections. Article 1 has allowed many unfair voting practices to be removed, but Americans must still be on the lookout for any unfair limits on their right to vote.

States across the nation have their own requirements for presidential voting as well. For example, in some states, convicted **felons** can vote, while in others they cannot.

PATH TO THE PRESIDENCY

IN VERMONT, SOMEONE CONVICTED FOR FIRST-DEGREE MURDER COULD VOTE IN 2018, WHILE IN MISSISSIPPI, SOMEONE WHO COMMITTED PERJURY—TELLING A LIE IN COURT AFTER PROMISING TO BE TRUTHFUL—COULD NOT.

In November 2018, Florida voters approved a historic measure that would give felons the right to vote—but another measure, passed in May 2019, states they must first pay back any fines and fees to the courts.

DECIDING ON THE DAY

Many Americans mark their calendars for the U.S. presidential elections. You may wonder: How was the date decided for a decision that affects so many people?

Today, presidential elections are held in every state at the same time: every four years on the Tuesday after the first Monday in November.

PRESIDENTIAL VOTING, 1800s

PATH TO THE PRESIDENCY

BEFORE A FEDERAL LAW PASSED IN 1845, STATES HAD A 34-DAY WINDOW IN DECEMBER TO HOLD PRESIDENTIAL ELECTIONS. BUT THIS MEANT THAT VOTING RESULTS MIGHT BE REVEALED BEFORE THE END OF THE VOTING PERIOD, AFFECTING VOTER TURNOUT.

Wednesdays didn't historically work for presidential elections because on that day of the week, most farmers brought their crops to markets to sell.

Early November was chosen because, with the nation's many farmers, spring or summer elections might interfere with planting and harvesting. People still relied on horses for travel in the mid-1800s, so a date later in the year wouldn't work in places with harsh winters. Finally, a Tuesday was chosen to give people time to get to their polling places after going to church on Sundays.

TIME TO VOTE!
HOW TO REGISTER

When you're old enough and ready to make your mark on history, it's not just the election date you must consider—you must also be registered to vote in time. In most states, you need to be registered somewhere from 10 to 27 days before Election Day.

To register, you must complete a National Mail Voter Registration Form. You can get it at state or local election offices and other public facilities such as libraries and schools. You can also register to vote from home by downloading a form available at eac.gov. On National Voter Registration Day, the fourth Tuesday in September, social media outlets including Snapchat, Twitter, and Facebook often promote shareable links to websites where you can register.

PATH TO THE PRESIDENCY

THE FEDERAL GOVERNMENT'S NATIONAL VOTER REGISTRATION ACT OF 1993, ALSO CALLED "MOTOR VOTER," REQUIRES THAT STATES ALLOW CITIZENS TO REGISTER TO VOTE WHEN COMPLETING OTHER PAPERWORK AT STATE MOTOR VEHICLE AND SOCIAL SERVICE AGENCIES.

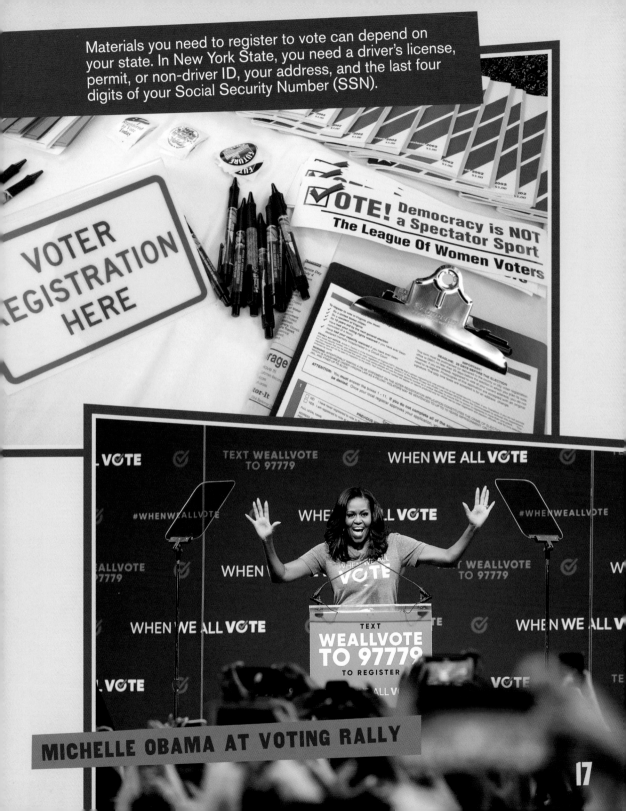

Materials you need to register to vote can depend on your state. In New York State, you need a driver's license, permit, or non-driver ID, your address, and the last four digits of your Social Security Number (SSN).

MICHELLE OBAMA AT VOTING RALLY

THE IMPORTANT PRIMARY PROCESS

Being president is a desirable job, so who decides which names make it on the ballot? The presidential primary process, run by states, makes this possible. Before the general election, both major **political parties** hold primary elections and caucuses that are part of this process.

Primary elections are similar to the general election in that people vote for their preferred presidential candidate via secret ballots. Caucuses, on the other hand, involve large gatherings of people in public places with **passionate** speeches in support of certain candidates. Both primary elections and caucuses determine which delegates will go to national conventions to represent their states. At national conventions, the political parties finalize candidates for president based on which candidate receives a majority of their party's delegate votes.

PATH TO THE PRESIDENCY

BOTH PRIMARIES AND CAUCUSES CAN BE OPEN OR CLOSED. WHEN THEY'RE OPEN, IT MEANS PEOPLE FROM ANY POLITICAL PARTY CAN VOTE. WHEN THEY'RE CLOSED, YOU MUST BE REGISTERED WITH THAT POLITICAL PARTY TO PARTICIPATE.

The Iowa caucuses, held earlier than others, are widely viewed as important indicators of a candidate's success in being nominated to run for their party in the general election.

WHAT HAPPENS AT A CAUCUS?

POLITICAL PARTIES ORGANIZE CAUCUSES, WHICH ARE OFTEN COLORFUL AND LOUD EVENTS HELD IN OPEN, PUBLIC SPACES SUCH AS SCHOOL GYMS AND TOWN HALLS. THEY USUALLY LAST SEVERAL HOURS. WHEN PEOPLE ARRIVE, THEY SORT INTO GROUPS BASED ON THE CANDIDATE THEY SUPPORT. SPEAKERS IN THE GROUPS THEN TRY AND CONVINCE MORE PEOPLE TO JOIN THEIR GROUP. THE GROUP WITH THE MOST PEOPLE AT THE END OF THE EVENT WILL RECEIVE THE MOST DELEGATE VOTES.

THE POWER OF THE POLLING PLACE

Presidential primaries, caucuses, and national conventions often receive extensive news coverage. After political parties have their candidates selected, voters must start planning their voting process on Election Day.

First, it's important to know where to go. When you register to vote, you're assigned to a polling place based on the address you gave when you registered. Usually, this is somewhere nearby in your community. Almost any large public space can work. Some common locations include community centers, government buildings, and even shopping malls. Often, these locations are in heavily trafficked areas along public transportation routes to make it easier for people to get to them. Most polling places also have parking and police on hand to help control traffic during peak voting periods.

PATH TO THE PRESIDENCY

POLLING PLACES HAVE SPECIFIC HOURS IN EACH STATE, OFTEN AROUND 7 A.M. TO 8 P.M. VOTERS MAY BE DISCOURAGED WHEN THEY FIND A LONG LINE, BUT POLLING PLACES MUST STAY OPEN UNTIL THE LAST PERSON WHO GOT IN LINE DURING POLLING HOURS HAS VOTED.

Polling places are often clearly marked with "Vote Here" signs.

A (MOSTLY) PAINLESS PROCESS

The process of voting only takes a few minutes, and technology is making voting increasingly easier. When using paper ballots, voters often fill them out behind a cardboard screen that keeps their selections private. Voters then file their ballots using an optical or digital scanner.

Instead of filling out paper ballots, some voters may make their selections on a screen using a Direct-Recording Electronic (DRE) voting machine. This machine remembers voters' choices. Another kind of voting machine used is a Ballot Marking Device (BMD). Like a DRE, this machine shows voters their choices on a computer screen and voters will mark their choices. However, it doesn't remember the selections and instead prints them out so they can either be hand-counted or scanned by a different machine.

PATH TO THE PRESIDENCY

FOR VOTERS WITH DISABILITIES WHO CAN'T EASILY LEAVE THEIR CARS, SOME STATES OFFER "CURBSIDE VOTING." THIS INVOLVES A POLL WORKER BRINGING A BALLOT AND OTHER VOTING MATERIALS TO THE VOTER'S CAR.

EARLY-BIRD AND ABSENTEE VOTING

DID YOU KNOW YOU CAN VOTE FOR PRESIDENT EVEN IF YOU'RE NOT IN THE COUNTRY? THIS IS POSSIBLE WITH ABSENTEE VOTING, WHICH ALLOWS YOU TO VOTE BY MAIL. THOUGH EVERY STATE HAS ABSENTEE VOTING, THE RULES VARY FROM STATE TO STATE. SOME STATES ALSO ALLOW EARLY VOTING IN PERSON BEFORE ELECTION DAY OR BY MAIL. BALLOT DROP-OFF STATIONS MAY BE AVAILABLE, AND SOME STATES ALLOW VOTERS TO RETURN MAIL BALLOTS TO POLLING PLACES ON ELECTION DAY.

Most states have laws requiring you to show some form of identification, or ID, before voting. Many states will only accept IDs with photos, such as driver's licenses and passports.

LAWS OF THE LAND

Polling places in the late 19th and early 20th centuries were often loud and unruly. Men would proclaim their political views and sometimes there were even brawls, or fights. In 1912, the state of Minnesota passed a law that prevented voters from wearing political buttons or other marks of their political views. This was among many steps states took to make voting more peaceful.

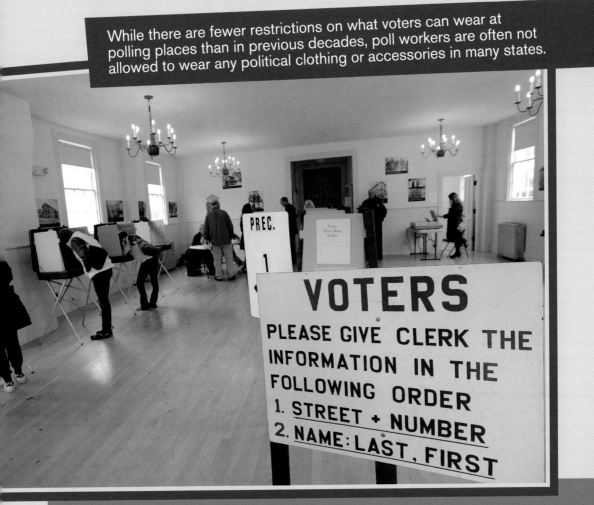

While there are fewer restrictions on what voters can wear at polling places than in previous decades, poll workers are often not allowed to wear any political clothing or accessories in many states.

PREC.
1

VOTERS
PLEASE GIVE CLERK THE
INFORMATION IN THE
FOLLOWING ORDER
1. STREET + NUMBER
2. NAME: LAST, FIRST

However, this raised a concern that's still often discussed today: Do these types of laws limit freedom of speech in polling places? In June 2018, the Supreme Court ruled that they do. Chief Justice John Roberts issued this opinion, stating the main issue was that the Minnesota law didn't specify what voters can wear and what they can't.

E-VOTING ON THE WAY?

While voting is already a fairly simple process, it can come with problems, such as having to drive to a voting place or waiting in line for hours at a time. With so many other activities, such as grocery shopping, moving online, why not vote online as well?

"E-voting," as it's commonly called, is being considered, but there are serious concerns with its security. Many worry it could cause voters to give up some of their privacy, and it may lead to more cases of voter fraud. In addition, following Russia's interference in the 2016 presidential election, U.S. officials are exploring ways to make elections more secure, such as offering top-secret security **clearances** to election officials at the state level.

PATH TO THE PRESIDENCY

ABOUT 42 COUNTRIES USE AN ONLINE AND ELECTRONIC VOTING SYSTEM CALLED "SCYTL" FOR AT LEAST ONE PART OF THEIR VOTING PROCESS.

Technology has improved our voting process and made it faster. Advanced technology is still being researched for secure online voting.

THE ELECTORAL COLLEGE DEBATE

The Founding Fathers saw the Electoral College as a compromise for the country's citizens. This was a compromise between the people choosing the president through popular vote or the option of Congress—the House of Representatives and the Senate—choosing the nation's leader.

In 2013, a national poll found about 63 percent of Americans would support a law that did away with the Electoral College. Those against it say it can limit voter turnout because voters wonder how much their votes count, and state leaders are successfully chosen without an Electoral College system. But the Electoral College's supporters say it helps give small states with lower populations an equal voice. Without the Electoral College system, many fear presidential candidates would hardly ever visit these small states, and thus their issues may go unheard.

PATH TO THE PRESIDENCY

OVER THE PAST 200 YEARS, MORE THAN 700 PROPOSALS HAVE BEEN INTRODUCED IN CONGRESS TO CHANGE OR GET RID OF THE ELECTORAL COLLEGE—MORE THAN ANY OTHER SUBJECT.

HILLARY CLINTON

DONALD J. TRUMP

The 2016 election marked the fifth time a candidate won the popular vote but lost the election based on electoral votes.

BOOST THE RATE: PARTICIPATE!

Voting participation in the United States remains low for a democratic country of its size and influence. When it comes to showing up on Election Day, 60 percent of the population votes. That may not sound too bad, but consider this: in countries with **compulsory** voting—which include Australia, Chile, and Belgium—about 90 percent of **eligible** voters cast votes in 21st-century elections. Even countries that have less strict voting policies, such as Austria, Sweden, and Italy, have voter turnout around 80 percent.

If you aren't old enough to vote, you can still encourage older family members and friends to go out to the polls. You can also pay attention to issues that you'd like a president to change. The continued success of our democracy depends on you!

PATH TO THE PRESIDENCY

THE U.S. CENSUS BUREAU HAS COLLECTED DATA THAT SHOWS IN 2014, ABOUT 21.4 PERCENT OF ELIGIBLE VOTERS WERE NOT REGISTERED TO VOTE.

GLOSSARY

amendment: A change in the words or meaning of a law, often in the U.S. Constitution.

clearance: When someone has permission to do something after an official decision is made.

compulsory: Required by a rule or law.

Constitutional Convention: A convention such as the one held in Philadelphia in 1787, at which representatives from each of the 13 colonies, except Rhode Island, decided how the United States Constitution would be written.

democracy: A government elected by the people, directly or indirectly.

discriminatory: Treating a person or group unfairly because of a perceived difference.

eligible: Able to be chosen or to participate.

felon: Someone who has committed a serious crime called a felony.

fraud: The crime of lying to take something of value from another person.

intimidation: Making other people feel afraid on purpose.

invalidate: To destroy or weaken the effect of something, or to make it no longer valid.

passionate: Expressing or showing strong emotions or beliefs.

political parties: Organizations of people who have similar beliefs about how power should be used, such as through policy-making, in a society or country. The two main parties in the United States are the Republican and Democratic Parties.

INDEX

WEBSITES

Due to the changing nature of Internet links, PowerKids Press has developed an online list
of websites related to the subject of this book. This site is updated regularly.
Please use this link to access the list: www.powerkidslinks.com/uspe/voting